# Pity the World

*Poems*

*Selected & New*

Bruce Taylor

Plain View Press
P. O. 42255
Austin, TX 78704

plainviewpress.net
sbright1@austin.rr.com
1-512-441-2452

Copyright Bruce Taylor, 2005.
All rights reserved.
ISBN: 1-891386-52-2
Library of Congress Number: 2005909034


Cover Photo: Charles Bass

*Pity the world, or else this glutton be.*

Sonnet One, William Shakespeare

# Acknowledgements

*Abraxus, Calliope, Chariton Review, Gulf Coast, The Anglican Theological Review, The California Quarterly, The Chicago Review, The Chicago Tribune, The Cumberland Review, The Exquisite Corpse, The Formalist, Greensboro Review The Hamline Journal, Hayden Ferry Review, The Journal, Light, Literary Salt, The Little Magazine, Madison Review, The Mankato Review, The Midwest Review, The Nation, The New York Quarterly, The New Orleans Review, New Works Review, NG, The Northwest Review, Passages North, Poetry Magazine, Poetry Northeast, Poetry Now, Poetry Superhighway, Porcupine, Savoy, Slow Trains, South Florida Review, The Texas Review, The Wisconsin Academy Review, Windfall, Windhover, Wisconsin Poets Calendar, The Wisconsin Review, Wisconsin West.*

"Calling It the Given," "Like," "Arabesque," and "Gray Drapes" first appeared in *Poetry* © 1994 by the Modern Poetry Association.

*The Best of 20 Years of Cream City Review* (Cream City Review), *Cross-Connect: The Best of 1997* (University of Pennsylvania), *Intimate Kisses: Poetry of Sexual Pleasure* (New World Press), *Patterns of Poetry: An Encyclopedia of Poetic Forms* (L.S.U. Press) *In My Neighborhood: Poetry of Wisconsin Cities* (Friends of Wisconsin Press), *Northwest Review: Thirtieth Anniversary Issue* (University of Oregon), *Slow Trains* (Samba Mountain Press), *Split Verse: Poetry of Separation and Divorce.* (Midmarch Arts), and *Wisconsin Poetry* (Wisconsin Academy of Arts and Sciences). *Upriver* (Upriver Press).

Poems and early versions of poems from this collection have also appeared in the following: *Everywhere the Beauty Gives Itself Away*, Red Weather Press, 1976; *Idle Trade: Early Poems*, Wolfsong Press, 1979; *This Day*, Juniper Press 1993; *Why That Man Talks That Way*, Upriver Press, 1994.

Copyright © 1976, 1979, 1982, 1984, 1993, 1994, 2005 Bruce Taylor.

# Contents

## from These Days (1993 -     )     9

Sunday     11
Blanket Weather     12
Next Door, Spring     13
Our Back Yards     14
January: Sunny and Cold: The Bus     15
Lately He's Been Trying To Not Be . . .     16
The Parents: The Photo     18
Middle-Aged Men, Leaning . . .     20
The Parable of the Pig and the Apple     22
Closet Poems     *sotto voce*     23
Envy     24
The Inside Cat     25
Middle-Aged Man, Sitting     26
Next Door     27
Wednesday, The Hole     29
Sunday, The Ordeal     30
Humming the 'B' Sides     31
Another Year, the Birds     32
From the Notebooks of Cabin 3     34
Hook Line and Sinker     38

## from *Firewatch* (1986)     39

Work and Prayer     41
The Long Straight     48

## from Living Like Thugs (1979 -     )     53

Rising Out Of Love     55
'Older' Guys Sing "The Stones"     56
Frank     57
Middle-Aged Man, Walking     59
Definitions Of a Kiss     60
The Secrets Of a Kiss     61
Errata     62
Ars Brevis, Vita Longa     63

    Photos of Poets    64
    What They Can and Cannot Fake    65
    What They Have and Have Not    66
    Almost Dancing    68
    Gossip: A Fiction    69
    La Chagalitte    70
    Evening Wind: Drawing and Print    72
    His Uncle Pearl    74
    That Kind of a Guy    76
    His Father Before Him    77
    His Good Felt Hat    78

## from *The Encyclopedia of Gardening (1995)*    81

## from *This Day* (1976-  )    89

    Foreigner    91
    The Window    92
    Gray Drapes    93
    Calling It the Given . . .    94
    Like    95
    Pathetique    96
    After Bonnefoy    97
    The Guest Room    98
    The Lesson    99
    Counting    100
    The Idea of Soul    101
    Bay View    *for Charlie*    102
    Bay View    103
    Children    104
    Then    106
    Strophe    107
    At the End Of the Road    108
    Forgetting    109
    Shame    110
    Mine    111
    For Dancing    112
    Arabesque    113
    A Whole Day    114
    Poem    115
    Lament    116
    **About the Author**    117

for Patti, Noah, Laura & Dan
for Hal Delilse, Jim Whitehead, Miller Williams
for my friends, they know who they are

**from These Days (1993 -      )**

*"We lived for days on only food and water."*

W.C. Fields.

# Sunday

Nobody goes to church much anymore,
though no one does much of anything else
so it's quiet, or as quiet as it gets;

usually there's a saw or somebody's mower,
a drill or a hammer hating another
repair we will have to live with

and the rare home run from the ballpark
and the pulse and trailing whisper
of the sprinklers when it's dry

and old deaf Winslow's blind
old cocker spaniel winds itself up
short around the clothes pole again

and the soft – almost apologetic –
screen door's screech and slam,
the trash can's guilty clatter after dark.

# Blanket Weather

Burrowing deeper into bed
beneath quilts and comforters,
blankets, flannel sheets and spreads,
we breathe and dream

enduring the level stare
of the red fox frozen in its den,
tracks that follow you everywhere
through an immaculate silence

days too blue to breathe
that sometimes go so clear
you begin to believe
you can skate them,

nights, 30 below and falling,
if you move they ring like bells,
out there other lives are calling
we know are worse than ours.

# Next Door, Spring

The kid's two this year
and in a neon-pink snow parka
for although it is April
it's April in Wisconsin.

Her snow pants are maroon
and large enough for three
so she squats when she sits,
it would be too easy to say,
like some surprising flower
amongst dry mulch and piles
of last November's leaves.

But her grandmother does
plant her in the saffroned lawn,
and go inside a moment.
Someone is always watching here
from a stoop next door or through
a window from across the alley.

And when she comes back,
pointing at a robin shivering
on a frozen clothesline,
and when she says "Spring,"
to the child blooming before her,
she's right of course.

Even in here, behind the grimy
storm-windows, even the inside plants
hunched in corners and clinging to
their few handfuls of dirt,
stir as if remembering.

## Our Back Yards

all face each other here so
whatever we have to hide we fail to.
She appears in a clean apron
among her chrysanthemums
and stands, hands on her hips,
while he reads the Trib
in the shade, everyone who knows
him says you'd never know
the Doctors say the cancer's worse.

Soon she is out running a wet rag
along her clothesline under a vaguely
threatening sky. Sanka in one hand,
a Lucky Strike tight in her mouth.
WAYY's on her kitchen radio
and her kitchen window's open.
September is 'Nostalgia Month'
and sometimes we're almost ashamed
at how little it takes to make us happy.

# January: Sunny and Cold: The Bus

It's not a long walk except its cold,
but sunny, so some try it and we pass them,
huffing their shadows, hands over their ears.
No news is good news and there's no news here.

She's quite a talker, we say after she's left,
busy about a Tuesday's bills and errands
getting off where she always does
at an alley where an oil truck is usually idling.

So we talk about that all the way downtown,
a son on each coast who take turns calling
every other Sunday and her daughter married
and divorced two or three times by now.

Our stout soprano driver sings "I'm in the Mood
for Love" over cobblestone and railroad track,
her raucous vibrato across pot-hole and frost-heave
takes us where she's going, and will bring us back.

# Lately He's Been Trying To Not Be
### *so sentimental about things*

The shirt his first wife
sewed for him, too large now
and lately out of date again,
she cut out the pattern

from the Saturday paper
and pieced it together
all Sunday afternoon on the floor
while he put on a pot roast

and peeled some potatoes
in the kitchen they had painted
on a whim the weekend before
an impish orange and yellow,

thinking even at that instant
how the small house must have looked
from outside, at a middle distance,
glowing in the November gloom.

Or the 8 x 10, pre-Kodacolor,
hand-tinted, "courting photo,"
as his father liked to call it,
where his parents were still together

and thought they always would be,
their arms lightly around each other
in some innocent gesture of
a tenuous, post-war intimacy,

on lawns tinged nostalgic green,
under the perfect weather
of a barefoot June, of Senior Prom,
of graduation, wedding, honeymoon

*continued*

where people pledged not lightly
to always love one another
and smiled into each other's faces
as if that's all that mattered.

# The Parents: The Photo

They are together there and
thought they always would be,
you can see it in his eyes.
He's cool in white bucks and
a sky blue windbreaker slung
over his shoulder lounging
outside of Somerville High.

Class on the high-hat and
barely 4-F he could polish off
and old soft shoe smoother
than any out of work hoofer
could tap an idle toe to,
the better joints still
echo his restless solos.

Buttery fleshed
rare ration of joy,
in war scared Boston
every liberty was hers
when all the adolescent soldiers
and all the sailor boys sailed off
to beat the Fascists back.

Coy acrobat but hip enough
to tease, she didn't go
all the way but went
pretty far and thought
she'd done OK for a girl.
Unaware the Russians
entered Warsaw, he told her
he'd call her again and did.

*continued*

A chesty little redhead
in a flashy cotton print that
shows a lot of leg for '45,'
tiptoed on five-inch spikes
and wearing a ten inch bow
that couldn't even then
have ever been that blue.

# Middle-Aged Men, Leaning
*four movements*

~
They lean on rakes.
It's late, it is evening
already inside their houses.

The children are gone.
Their wives are on the phone
talking softly to someone else.

This frost, this early Fall
upon their minds, a small
measure of patience and regard

as if the twilight world
in bright papery pieces
diminished so and thus.

~
They lean on hoes
in Spring the green earth
turned once more beneath them

their eyes full of flowers
their hands full too
of the planting still to do

the weeds and drought awaiting
their pocketful of seed
the water they must carry.

*continued*

~
In an early winter dark they lean
on shovels, a graying heart
a last bad rap inside them,

looking upward toward the sky
the yard, the driveway, the car
the street, the world

itself for all they know
buried by the falling snow
even as they gasp to breathe

and re-breathe the visible breath,
like a burst cartoon balloon
of an old imperfect prayer.

~
In summer, after long mowing,
they lean toward a growing
silence in the plush grasses

in leaves of many greens
in trees of their own colors
where grackle and crow

each to its own shadow
in the dusky reach of branches
gather quietly to stay.

# The Parable of the Pig and the Apple

*And if thy sowe have moo pygges than thou wilt rere,
sell them or eate them.*
                              Fitzherb 1586

That pig
that rough snout of arrogance
that happy as a pig in shit pig
that brick pig that straw and twig pig
pig of my heart

This little pig blind little jug
the wee wee one
that much maligned pig
that slow big dirty lazy
fat as a pig pig that swine

The eater and shitter
that thunder-pig bearer of rain
the iron sow the goddess
the old white one
that great mother of a pig
the shining one

The Lunar Pig that cannibal that
Sarazan Christian Muslim Hindu Pig
that money in the bank pig
the one in a poke
the eater the eater
that rude calling
swill pig swill pig

That stuck pig, the squealing one,
that roast pig, that apple in its mouth
that sweet sweet candied apple.

# Closet Poems
*sotto voce*

~

Without you he's ridiculous.
No matter the scarf's savoir faire,
the hat's panache,
without you on the subway,
he's arrested, penniless,
locked out without you.
Without you what do the hands do,
hanging around? Pants,
this morning, he puts you on again.

~

You whose arms embrace
as a favorite lover would,
that button with five new moons.
Two pockets for cigarettes or pens
but rarely a wallet and never the hands.
Stain he pretends is blood but is jam.
Loose ghost, soft shell, shirt
he wakes to rise to fill you up.

~

Old shoe, old wife,
he's dreamed inside you
the footless life.
Soft-tongued, frayed lace,
sometimes dancer, shoe,
you angel you, in winter,
or out among the doggy world,
who could do without you,
both of you?

# Envy

is the meanest sin
but it's all you have left.
Lust, of course, you spent it

by the handful. You've had
your fill of Gluttony and lately
sleep right through Sloth.

Wrath passes. Your's anyway.
And avarice is only greed
for what other people have.

You no longer take any Pride
in being beyond all that
but even the dead, you imagine,

envy.

# The Inside Cat

Sometimes you hate the Inside-Cat,
it depends on you for everything.
You lug its food in the front door
and haul its litter out the back.

Deaf for years in at least one ear,
half-blind, as far you can tell,
it eats nothing that you buy it
and shits anywhere at all.

Snug on winter's woolen lap,
or the coolest sill to lie through June,
by now it sleeps through everything,
has gone to gray, to gristle and fat.

Sometimes, at night, the windows
are the faces of the Inside-Cat,
howling at black handkerchiefs of bats,
staring at moonlit rabbits in the snow.

## Middle-Aged Man, Sitting

He never felt bad much until he was forty
then guilt arrived one evening.
It was as old as you would expect,
with a bad cough, and it sat
on the edge of the chair
with its face in its trembling hands
the way his father always sat.

The next years it was greed,
streaking in a classic black Porsche
through another long weekend,
a strange young woman riding shotgun,
sexual acrobats in sequined Danskins
working high without a net.

Tonight, on the back stoop,
after dinner with a warm beer
in one hand and the hose in the other,
watering what left of the honeysuckle
and watching the swallows swoop
and dive beyond his neighbor's roofs,

he imagines his regret tomorrow,
going through the trash in the alley,
choosing what there is to choose
and keep from what he had thought
he was only throwing away but no,
he knows now how it is taken,
piece by dreaded piece.

# Next Door

Wasn't this what he wanted this
living with and making do,
whose trick's to stay unfinished
and turn out well, or hope to.

The lawn, his public labor,
gone shamelessly
to dandelion and clover,
the vegetable plot
to fir and yew.

He was drunk on quarts
six days a week by noon
and shortly after Church
every Sunday on schnapps.

The spot where he grew
hollyhock she's had
paved over and sits there
looking a long afternoon
exactly as he used to.

To walk a little more surely
along the old uncertainties,
to live, if need be, obscurely
but long and in tranquility.

He'd be out before supper
on that rickety ladder
he had leaves in the gutters
and squirrels in the attic.

*continued*

Where love elevates the mundane
in the world and binds us to it,
where what remains, remains
at least familiar and compassionate.

The clothes-lines diminish
from four to two then one,
the abandoned skeleton
of a forgotten trellis
its random blossoms insists.

# Wednesday, The Hole

Isn't often you see a hole dug
as deep as this one up here so
when the county came to dig it
most of the old men came around
sometime during the day to watch.

So there were usually four
or five guys standing around
watching three guys standing around
watching one guy dig, and the boss
came by twice to check, and the Power
& Light guys stopped by too.

And the kids on their trikes,
painted red white & blue,
were warned "don't get too close"
but did and it was all too much
for Happy, Ray's penned-up
husky pup, who's learned to ignore
the tomcat's strut or another
fat rabbit fattening upon
clover in the patchy lawn.

Lunchtime, the crew took their pails
to the shady side of the truck
and someone brought ice-tea
and Ray smuggled them a beer each.
Then it was back to work so
a different guy dug and Ray took
the Buick to the Super-A
for popsicles and more beer.

## Sunday, The Ordeal

You forget how it can get here
but then it is August
and the pipes begin to sweat.
A fat kid tailed by his pimply sister
kicks a useless kite all up and down
another treeless street named Elm.

Or the catbird, low in the honeysuckle,
and the cat itself only half-dozing
on the garden wall by the newlyweds
next door who are no longer young,
but are close enough for this town.

Two alleys over there used to be
a mom and pop place until Pop died
and Mom boarded up the big windows,
took down the sign and went inside,
got sick and hasn't come out since.

Everything's sent in or taken out.
A hired guy from Social Welfare
does the lawn and shovels when
it snows but doesn't do the drive
and someone, maybe a son, stops by
Sundays in a cab but never stays long.

# Humming the 'B' Sides

*It's Autumn in New York*
as he vacuums, since his wife's got
the day job it's the least he can do,

or *What Is This Thing Called Love*
while he waits in the mini-van
for the kids after swimming or piano.

It's *Ebb Tide* when the cat, the baby,
the fat goldfish in the algaed pond
doze and float in a lazy eddy

of a August late afternoon nap,
and *They Can't Take That Away from Me*
later still when the tin little A.M. grins

dimly in the dusk tuned faintly to
WAYY, "where every tune's a memory,
where all the great old songs have gone."

## Another Year, the Birds

All summer long there was always
a caw, a complaint or call.
And later in the fall,
as the breathy clouds
when the wind's westerly move
endlessly away from you,
whole flocks of finch appeared
to forage in the weeds
that struggle and go to seed where
the driveway fractures and drifts,
as the continents themselves,
we are told, fracture and drift.

And in winter at 30 below,
your breath escaped you,
a white cloud across
that big morning star
like one singular and rare
chrome wind chime's note,
then a door far off slams so
another does then a dog barks
then another then the pickups,
cars and vans in sequence startle
the heavily feathered sparrows
flocking bare lilacs along
four geometric blocks
of perfectly shoveled snow.

*continued*

And then the same swallows come
back to nest in the same
inverted flower-pot painted
whatever color's handy
and nailed to a shingle
blown off the roof,
and then the trees take on
their burden again and again
we are left with almost nothing
but Spring and happiness,
the conditional joys.

# From the Notebooks of Cabin 3

> *you are incarnate in*
> *the world and we live*
> *caught up in you*

Teilhard de Chardin

> *the wicked are like the troubled sea*
> *when it can not rest*

Isaiah 57:20

> *one honeymoon day*
> *one honeymoon night*
> *nothing else to say*
> *nothing else to write*

Anonymous

Everyone mentions the "waves," of course,
and the "crying" of the gulls
and the "moon," through the one small window,
"full," "half," or otherwise
provocatively sickled against
a "starry" or "starless" sky,
or as Helen Rusted, of Fond du Lac, put it:

> *the thriving mysteries of life*
> *unfolding in waves of time*
> *spiriting through*
> *the vast existence in space*

Many honeymooned or re-honeymooned here,
most are thankful for the change
from whatever to whatever,
everyone goes on almost endlessly
about the peace and quiet.

*continued*

*we have been married four days*
*we love each other very much*
*didn't get seasick listening to the waves*
*through faith in the lord*
*we will be married forever*

*do we sound boring,*
*we don't think we are*

They had "wieners and cheese for breakfast" or
"crackers and cheese for breakfast lunch and dinner"
or "champagne and meatballs by candlelight"
or "picked blueberries for pancakes
and raspberries in big dishes with cream."

*had some nice fresh herring,*
*hot cookies and milk just out of the cold*

*in this just right cabin,*
*the carefully watched toast made*
*on the top of the stove*

The lake was a lullaby, or nt.
They loved or hated the bed
which was not "big enough for three"
according to "Don & the girls",
which was "noisy but
sure held up," "Figgy and Ray,"
in which they slept, if at all,
like a "stone" a "cloud", a lot of "logs"
a "baby" or "the dead."

*we found #3 by pure luck*
*almost got rammed by a semi*

*continued*

the evening of the 19th my wife
got stomach flu
and I got the regular flu
the day after that day

fell off the cliff
and lost my shoe but
it could have been worse

we came here to be alone
married three years already with a little girl
this Shawnee's hand print (slightly enlarged)
5 mos. old, 1st time anywhere

Mrs. Anthony Swanshera of St Paul
will be back "if I can talk my husband into it,"
and Ginny, Eddie, Lionda, Edvart and Tottsie
are planning to return, in three years,
"God willing"

we came to find ourselves once more
to remember that what we need
we have already in each other

we used to come here as children
now we have children
and grandchildren of our own
and we are still coming

we are in or 70's
and it makes a good honeymoon spot

we loved each other tenderly
and our fondness increased
as we grew old

*continued*

*I sat on the rocks, smoking,*
*and her reading to me*
*in the pleasing wild*

*Cassie found the notebooks*
*and as she read*
*years and faces came alive*

*it has been good*
*watching this plan unfold,*
*creating wholeness*
*in our life*

note: The quoted material was selected from a series of "guest books" dating back to 1937 found in a rental cabin in a small resort on the North Shore of Lake Superior. People were asked in the original notebook to write whatever they wanted, and provide another when the current one was full.

# Hook Line and Sinker

We toss open the shade
do the dishes while coffee
for the thermos brews,
check an iffy sky through
the small-paned window,

feed the sleepy cat,
grab the bait from the fridge
the pole from off the wall
and get on with it.

We are not fishers
of men but men fishing
what depths we do not know
casting not bread but flesh
across a mysterious surface

where small fry school
where fat carp loll
among lily pad and cattail
where the sudden pike lurks.

So the heart's weather
calms and storms
each day sets out
rudderless with anchor lost
its white promise unfurling

to hunt by touch to gather
what we can not see
our seed our bait
our hope for luck our tack.

# from *Firewatch* (1986)

*"I prayed to you in the daytime with thoughts and reason, and in the nighttime you have confronted me, scattering thought and reason. I have come to you in the morning with light and with desire, and you have descended upon me with great gentleness."*

Thomas Merton (1915-1968)

# Work and Prayer

~

We are the choir indistinct
these rainy autumn afternoons
beyond the heavy doors
in the dark chapel
in the shadow of the water tower
where the old barn used to be.

The gray cornfield clay
from manuring before breakfast
clings and hardens on our feet.

Steel splinters,
the sparks of the big saw
we were out filing at dawn,
work into our palms their
sudden blessedness.

~

He catches me sleepy and happy
with little to do but pray
in the shade behind the church.
"Monks sweat!" Modestes, rarely
found where parables are spoken,
says so by pointing to our ancient
Brother Donatus in a straw hat
repairing the beleaguered trellis
sagging and full of roses
in the Novitiate's garden,

*continued*

by pointing to the Novitiates
themselves full of happy antiphons
practicing their sweet polyphony
between the garage and hog-shed
at the muddy edge of the pond,

by pointing to the steeple whose
topmost cross Brother Processus
painted with yellow traffic-paint,
swinging up there for days with
surely, his angels hanging on to him.

~
Silence has put all
the noises of the day away,
each to its unspoken place.
You will hear no complaint
from the weary floor,
the hypocrite door.

Neither will the single
shrill tea kettle's note
insist itself for now.

The corner takes back
its stares, the chairs their
sighing and goings forth,

the long, pale rows of tables
set as in a dream, awaiting something,
our postulant bowls set out
as always early before sleep.

*continued*

~
Little Father John-of-God, tossing
in the bell-ringer's corner
next to Modestes who names
each of his tomato plants after a saint.

Our blacksmith, Brother Abel,
who works with a hammer
in one hand and a rosary
in the other, the beads
run through his blackened fingers
while the iron is in the fire.

Dosithieus Leroi who goes nowhere
nor does nothing unless
bidden by another, who will stand
all day and think of God,
who sleeps in the draftiest hallway
on precisely four handfuls of straw.

Have you ever knelt down
alone in the dark and pled
to be let go? Have you listened
to the walls at this hour?
Have you heard their generations
of unutterable prayer?

~
Here to the top of the tower
where the night is wonderful
I come in winter after dinner
full of sleep and potatoes

*continued*

to walk with the lamp
that is always a question
always the same thing
it listens and says nothing.

Some will not name you out of
fear, awe, oblation, meekness,
I too have been steeped
in all of these because to me
you have so many names –

blue, sky blue, too blue
not to praise across the sad ecru
and gray of moonlit planes –
every other color, every shade
tint tinge and hue –

thin serenade a wind like this
sings as it settles in long grasses
in breathy ferns that
rise up beneath the moon

white chapel spire,
willow silver in the evening,
plush mosses
seas of holiness and prayer
upon whom mercy falls.


~
Free to pray
today and happy in a way
that does not want to talk,
I have not really "thought"
of much of anything for hours.

*continued*

No matter how simple
our talk or thought may be
it is never simple enough.

The true prayer is listening,
the heart at its stations
systole and diastole –

the red wasps at the sunny wall of the church
the catbird mocking in the cedar tree
the hummingbird caught in the cloister

and in the empty choir-loft where
the jubilant dead sit up to sing
all about the presence of God.

~
I think i have prayed
because my knees are sore.

I think I have done
great things because
I am worn out.

I am afraid Processus kept
a better Lent than I did
Good Shepard Sunday.

I am nurse this week
because I am ill enough to be here
but not the illest in Infirmary.

Blessed as I am by
the odor of wet wool
and many grown men

*continued*

and the chance to minister to
Father Placid the Cellarer
who has eaten too many
of his own green apples.

~
When we rise the first
and the least of men
outside the walls of the world
we are as old metal
given to different sounds
the secret of many small bells
strongly pitched

the novices in their nightboots
and with their candles
who do not yet know
their psalms in the dark

the assistant cantor in
the warmest corner
at choir
who when the holy water
freezes in the fount
skims the thin ice, signing

"a good building praises God
better than a bad one."

*continued*

~
Yesterday after chapel, Modestes
who sometimes wakes me by
singing the *Veni Creator Spiritus*
very loudly in his sleep
took me to the barnyard
for the blessing of the animals.
As this month's rectory second-servant,
I had to go to say my prayers
and then put out the soup

but first the shy calves in the calf pen,
then the indifferent sheep.
The chickens we could not catch
we blessed on the wing.
The rabbits stood still
for our censer and incense
but shivered when we dropped
the holy-water on them.

Even the devils, Modestes says,
deserve God, so we chased
a few apostate ducks through
the ragged fence he'll have me
mending the next day, or the next.

# The Long Straight

*Nullabor, W.A. Australia*

~
We people the earth where the earth
allows us: this is the lesson
of the desert and the city.

Whatever green there is is small,
stunted, hugs the ground: scrub
saltbush, mulga and saltgrass.

Where there's so little the little
there is means much; the mind
makes what it can from what there is.

Here and there beside the track,
a sign – no people,
no building, hill or valley –

only the native names for the minimal:
*Naretha, Wilban, Mungalla, Malbooma:*
*Saltbush, Cave, Sandrift, Wind.*

~
When even words give out, we slow,
cautious of this human trespass,
uncertain what is moving, uncertain
even more of what is standing still.

Even the birds give up,
miles back, the last black insult
of crow, the final parrot
in a lone gum tree, a solitary kite
spiraling the limit of its range.

*continued*

The eye seeks without relief
the detail to justify itself.
Far enough away a patch of scrub
could be kangaroo or even emu but
never human, too ridiculous to assume.

~

This mile, moment, step –
enormous and meaningless –
abandoned with the other creatures
of the air, dust-devil, mirage,
windsweep and regret.

The sky goes a subtler blue now,
one cloud far off and thin.
The stars, not one by one as they do
above the guilty city, but all at once
are out to wonder and amaze.

There is no counting of stars here,
no picking one to wish on,
nor are they fixed to point to
as above the troubled seas;
here they swirl, streak and blaze
across such emptiness only darkness
claims it, and only for awhile.

~

It is the eye that's thirsty now
and the thirsty eye looks to itself
and the heart that beats, beats
both ways, then and now, self and other.

*continued*

The eye becomes the horizon.
The hand touch, tool and missile.
The span of many steps the distance to cross.
The ear the sound and seeker of sound
until the voice in silence longing
breathes in the darkness and speaks.

~
In the dreaming time the sky heroes
lived with their dog-footed wives
and many sons and daughters
chasing clouds all day for water.
In the dreaming time all was journey
and becoming. The sun and the moon,
the she and the he shined together in
the sky which was all colors all the time.

~
Over the hard ground where the emu run,
over the field of clay-pan where water
may rest after rain, through the belly of light
past anthills along the sand hill Rainbow-Snake made

when it arched its back, over ground studded with stones
to the plane of smaller, sharper stones for cutting,
past good firesticks, past chisel and hammer-stones
past wodika and kaylu, wira and nardoo

past the white mounds – wives of brothers mourning –
to the valley where the Mura-Mura yawned
to the small salt lake – white-patch – where
Dorama's dog who wore a white patch
was killed by a kangaroo and buried

*continued*

to the place where the goanna hide from the sun
by the caves where Native-Companion danced
when she came back to earth and it rained

and a great mob of flowers bloomed in the wind
and the women laughed with their laps full of seed.

**from Living Like Thugs (1979 -    )**

*"Is it hot in here, or am I crazy."*

                Charlie Manson

# Rising Out Of Love

He looked up at the moon, pieces of which
were then touring Arkansas.
He picked out a dozen stars
that didn't resemble fresh wept tears.
He looked up 'lips' in an unabridged dictionary.

He imagined her in other contexts:
waltzing with hubby, biting her nails
during *As the World Turns*,
feeding fries to three kids at McDonalds.
He imagined her as she was – unconcerned.

He tried to dwell on her bad points,
the turkey-skin behind her knees,
the lingering odor of Lavoris and Noxema,
the slightly off-blue, no, azure eyes
of some lousy tipper who
never remembers his name.

# 'Older' Guys Sing "The Stones"

*". . . imagining the world that I got"*

A Salesman on a lucky roll
his profit is your loss.
The Dentist on a weekend prowl
his pockets full of floss.

The Gravedigger out for a laugh.
The Shrink for a shoulder to cry on.
The Plumbers on time and a half.
The Bankers who never will buy one.

The Painter who knocked off early
today and may tomorrow too.
The Guys who had it made, nearly,
and Guys that don't know it but do.

The Little Guys on the tall stools.
The Fat Guys bellied up to the bar.
The Young Guys trying to be so cool
and the Old Guys so sure that they are.

# Frank

*"You make me feel so young"*

He tries to act like twenty-two
all sap and spastic charm
when he's around you
it works, he thinks, but then

someone in a barroom mirror
does an ugly double-take
and there's that forty year
old fat guy on the make

again, that froggy clown
that roly-poly Romeo,
that snaggle-toothed Don Juan,
that sad and sleepy Cyrano

to your Juliet, jejune,
your Isolde as ivory ingenue
in waiting to the moon,
ever renewing and ever renewed.

"I'd even be forty for you,"
you say with exaggerated dread,
but then he'd be sixty-two
and unconcerned, perhaps, or dead.

Of what exactly should he inform
your beautiful youth
almost ever eager in his arms?
Certainly not the truth

*continued*

which is it's not he is
too old to play this part
but that by now he is,
or ought to be, too smart.

So he plans to leave, maybe,
walk off alone out into the cold,
right after "One for my Baby
and One More for the Road."

## Middle-Aged Man, Walking

He knows the world is round
they said so in school
but he walks it flatly still,
an edge more than horizon.

Not as you might walk a planet
rolling around a universe
you fear to suppose or even infer
but as you plot and replot

a trip on a map so creased
and wrinkled each section
threatens if you check it again
to fracture off into pieces.

A languid idle by the river
Summer Spring and Fall
or the Winters' trackless stroll
over one bridge and back another.

Streets that rush off to work
and come straight home
that amble to the tavern
and tangle eventually back.

The burn in the calf or the shin,
the stab in the back or the chest,
the lack of the little breath left,
the journey uphill or down.

# Definitions Of a Kiss

To touch or caress with the lips,
an expression of sweet affection,
greeting, respect or amorousness;
or to touch lightly, a connection

gently, as in *flowers kissed
by dew*. To strike, lightly, brush
against as in I barely *missed
the other dancer's ample tush*.

A piece of candy, chocolate.
In pool, a glance or carom
*Slang*. To dismiss or reject.
To be forced to give up on.

As in to *kiss goodbye* or *kiss off*,
to osculate, canoodle or to buss.

# The Secrets Of a Kiss

could mean many things, for instance
what kisses do or do not tell –
the eloquence of their reticence–
or how to do it, kiss, that is, well.

The kiss as punctuation: period,
question or even exclamation
as addenda or *abracadabra,*
an act of goodbye or consummation.

The one that says I'm leaving
but you don't know it yet
or the one that gets you believing
again what you want to forget.

The kiss that starts the heart aflutter,
the one you know will make it better.

# Errata

Wherever I said *her*, I meant *you*.
Wherever I said *him*, I meant *me*.
The skies were not always blue,
      he really wasn't everything to her,
he merely meant to be.

He only lied to protect her
from the worst he knew he could be.
She left him shortly thereafter,
      he started to smoke again,
and drink, and write a little poetry.

For *champagne* and *croissants*,
read *day-old bread* and *beer*.
Whenever, as he often does,
      he swears he's glad she's gone,
read instead, *I wish you were here*.

# Ars Brevis, Vita Longa

What fun to be the poet's son
and have your many praises sung.
How droll to be the subject of
tetrameter and doggerel.

How odd to be the painter's wife
a ready study, a model for life
to sit and wonder who does he see
after twenty years of living with me?

How cold to be the dancer's old flame
gone sullenly tone-deaf, heavy and lame
who once was partner, a friend, a lover
is now an excuse to dance with others.

## Photos of Poets

Taken in better light
or times by a lover,
former or about to be,
more given to epiphany
and excess, Gin & Lime,
mad passions and rages

still a guilty casualty
badly cropped
to some ancillary spot
up-stage right upon
their own back pages

a negative of the beautiful,
a emigre's bleak passport,
a candid portrait's
transparent grain and gloss
focused on some future
developing promise lost.

## What They Can and Cannot Fake

Any orgasm except a real one.
True love but not a sneeze
not at least convincingly so.
Death, as children make believe

though never nearly long enough.
And the shape of a kiss on the lips
but not the reach nor rest of touch
that lingers just below the finger tips.

Any present fashion of desire
lust's vogue and classic craze
but not the first loss loss requires,
nor compassion's passion ablaze.

Not luck or the Blues, a fugue, cold sweat,
foul fate, true tragedy or real regret.

## What They Have and Have Not

They have no snapshots
they might ever keep
together except the secret
fleeing ones they take

in passing neon barroom
windows or lingering
in steamy motel mirrors
on which he paints for her

in operatic opiates awash
in letters clearly enduring
the traditionally initialed heart
the tragic arrow recondite.

They are not often Saturday
mornings in the park nor on
a sinless Sunday afternoon
stroll a civil boulevard to talk.

They rarely get to shop much,
argue or nap, time's too
short to waste on anything but
how happy they can be together.

The room they move in is
just large enough for two
small windows painted shut
ugly drapes coarsely cut

somehow they make do,
her skirt a lovely puddle
on the floor by the door
where she skinned out of it

*continued*

his pants dancing off the chair
"You have to stop biting me,"
she reminds him, "where it shows."
And he agrees.

## Almost Dancing

Drunk on fine wine and the freedom to be
obvious over foreign coffees, cognac
and the just deserts of sin, it seemed in
this distant city among strangers with

all she was or was not wearing beneath
her new dress only he knowing though
anyone who watched even a giddy while
might have naughtily guessed or known by

furtive heart or remembered once the earthly
scent of motel soap and mortal pretense,
they could dance, they thought, in this place,
could nap or dine *al fresco* – do anything together

the word they've lately learned to use
for any place or time that makes them happy.
This far from home anything could happen
which is why they have to go this far

shrugging off some other life's gray array
too cheerless and heavy for a latitude
as wide and warm as this exotic parallel,
traveling on credit someone else will pay.

# Gossip: A Fiction

Do you know those lovers Haesip and Koepke?
Like two otters at a waterfall the two of them
the shame they should feel they don't.
To noon every Sunday their shutters go latched
and her poor dear so younger than him the fool
going out without a collar, flowers in his hat
falling in love like that, everyone watching.
Touching? I tell you there's no time they don't.
You'd think one honey one a bear I don't care which.
They've gained a stone between them lying around
in each other's arms as if that's all that mattered.
When he is at his awl, she sits beside him they say
reads as he mends from French Romances, out loud!
Four books they have now in the window in a row.
Sometimes they fight, and when they do she
screams such shrill such filthy things across
the yard, my sow bloats and goes off corn.
Drunk on Innocents, Koepke himself said red-headed
women buck like goats, then beat Hanaud for laughing
he couldn't ride a week, Koepke yelled back he'd build
new out near the bog, come to town now only for salt.
You know how her hair fires as she kneels waiting
on the beach for him his the last boat in as usual.
Sure plenty of young men call to her Haesip Haesip
are you a new girl we've not seen you for so long
and shake their jellies at her like they would burst.
And you know that big fish Koepke got him going out
so far everyone thought he'd never come back, he gave it
for a ribbon, told the tailor who told me not to tell.

# La Chagalitte

*"Why is the horse green?*
*Why is the cow flying in the sky?*
*What has this to do with Marx or Lenin?"*

Party Official

*Around Her*

Like bread made anew
another morning rises
the happy woman has
returned from the sun
her wicker unburdened
her cat sleeps curled
on her shirt on the floor

The seed in the apple
flowers above the orchard
the moment she plucks it
the beautiful day's official
even the sweet milk
pearls at her breast.

*Bella*

If every lover
leapt like you
quick to the eye's
ever weaving basket
then dancing is how
the world would work

There you are now
calling crops
into harvest
there you are again
a heavy fruited rain

*continued*

Roses bloom, bird song
nests in the heart
nests in the heart's nest.

*The Poet at 3 O'clock*

If the soldier in the snow's
that happy of course
his hat would float above
his upside-down head,
If a giant rooster played
a violin, it would be a blue one.

If the lovers at their windy promenade
were not aware of this apparition why
would they fly each other like kites?

*The Lovers at the Eiffel Tower*

I have been held like that,
close, high upon high places,
and filled with the moment
that rises and rises.

I have laid down
like that, blue spoons
upon a timeless river bank.

I too have knelt to listen
in the evening at
the slender throated lily.

I too have been swept away.

# Evening Wind: Drawing and Print

*after Hopper*

~
The window is open
and the woman is naked
at the foot of the bed
leaning towards the window
trying for the breeze.

The curtain is blown back
behind her over her shoulder,
the bed is rumpled from her
tossing all afternoon in the heat.

There is a pitcher of water
on the bedside table
and a picture of something
in a rectangular frame
centered upon the wall
directly behind her.

It is a landscape or
a horizon of the kind favored
by those who live in small
one-windowed rooms,
it is a still-life of sorts
and she has studied it for hours.

~
She was rising to refill
the pitcher on the table
when she felt his eyes upon her
as a sudden gust of wind tore back
the curtains from the window
and he saw she saw him staring.

*continued*

He turned around quickly,
walked on down the street,
looked back over his shoulder
just once to catch her leaning
just out far enough to see him go.

She is alone and not expecting
anyone or thing to change that.
She imagines him believing
she's left him for another
but she's left him for no one
and fears she may regret it.

# His Uncle Pearl

was a fat man with a thin mustache,
bad teeth and a funny hat,
who read three newspapers a day
and fell asleep on the couch,

a brute with a belt
and a hell of a backhand
a big pile of shit
or a shower of gold

a skinny chicken-legged
badly balding guy with
hardly any ass at all
jogging towards the 7-11
at 10:57 for Schlitz.

The guy at the bend
of a horse-shoe bar
peeling big bills off
a wad from his pocket,
lots louder than the rest.

The gut-gone loose shooter
eight-balling for beer,
one sly eye in the pocket
of every move the barmaid makes,
he'll snag her yet upon

his hooky smile, he thinks,
*That'll Be the Day*, she plays
back on the jukebox
*You Can't Always Get What You Want*.
The bleary old rummy, teary

*continued*

eyed in the mirror with
a couple of dollars left,
a sucker for the 'B' sides
maybe he'll play *It Happened
in Monterey*, maybe *Angel Eyes*,
one more time and leave.

## That Kind of a Guy

that cool silver-haired old dude
in the sharp black jacket
      and a spiffy pair of shoes –
in a tiny, gray and white, button-flap
      checkered cap and a pin in his lapel
who is always going somewhere
      running his errands, making the rounds

the kind of a guy has to
  draw pictures when he talks
on the back of napkin or
  scrawl something approximate
across a scrap of an envelope

      there's this letter to mail
and the Light Bill to pay
and the Buick to get gassed and washed,
      and the list his wife leaves
him everyday, and he's been looking
everywhere, he says, for a little
copper washer, 'about this big.'

"OK," he's always saying, "I got
to run, I got to go." The Optimist,
      the Moose or Shriner,
the Foreign Legionnaire, the Knight of Columbus,

who's always raffling off something
collecting something for
some worthy cause or another
      selling light bulbs for the blind
or paper flowers for the sleeping dead.

## His Father Before Him

was one of the quiet ones,
who spent most of his time
in the cellar or garage
from right after supper
until everyone else was asleep,
puttering around with something,
fixing this or that, fixing it again

who sat in the dark in the kitchen
with the last cold cup of coffee
and smoked and hummed and thought
with the radio on low and tuned
to somewhere far off, fading
in and out, scratchy, oddly
operatic static ridden and remote

a man who may have loved you
but never said it, a guy who meant well
but moody, bored, angry, tired, mute
in his male terror, huge,
hairlessly marbled, frontally nude,
smelling of whiskey and gasoline,
working too hard, dying too soon.

## His Good Felt Hat

All dogs and children awaiting
his flat ascending steps
up the steepest hill
for miles around,
hunched over, hands deep
into the jingle of his pockets

full of keys and key chain,
change purse, small change,
clean hanky, subway tokens, Tums
and Lifesavers or better yet,

Chicklets, or cough-drops, or gum
he'd give some to any grandchild
who could spell his word for the day
or who had learned another verse
from Proverbs or the Psalms

with his good felt hat in his hand
and his jacket folded neatly
over the other shoulder,
and his always white shirt
and his pin for perfect attendance
in the too wide lapel
of his second best suit

and his braces, belt
with initialed buckle,
vest, vest-chain, fob,
collar-stays, tie-pin,
cuff-links, Parker pen
and pencil set, glasses case,
address book and billfold

*continued*

and if it was a Sunday
his best blue suit
and his bible, the small one,
and a white boutonniere
for his mother who was dead
and the envelopes for the offering.

# from The Encyclopedia of Gardening (1995)

*If you would be happy for a week, take a spouse. If you would be happy for a season, kill a pig. But if you want to be happy forever, plant a garden."*

Chinese Proverb

*"...the garden remains a woman's idea"*

A plot of ground close to home
A fence of thorn and roses

Scrap of branch or bone
scapula or femur
Crotched stick or hoe of shell

Wild seed gathered
Meadow root dug and stored
Water carried throughout drought.

*"The good gardener plants for three,
maybe four years from now."*

In a garden like that there's
Always too much to do.
The maple he should have
Planted the day
His daughter was born
Would have been by now
Memento yellow

And through the kitchen door
She should be stepping
To shake some white thing
Or another and stand
Just a moment just so
The hollyhocks would have
Something lovelier to tower over

And tiger-lilies should be
Flashing shamelessly orange
And late asters in their
Final purple should be nodding
Thick and heavily-headed

*continued*

Against the garage he ought
To have painted last year,
Or the year before last,
Immaculately white.

*"gardening as a form of worship."*

To bring us to our knees
To bring us back to quiet
Inclined as we are
To this labor and attention

Where there's little
Choice but to begin
With the intensive
Care of the present

Grub up the dying
Start with something new
Deprive the bad
And nurture the good

Simple stuff it seems
At first, herbs drying,
A red flood ripening
Upon a cool and shady sill

The blue cold's cluster
In the morning glory vines,
The ardor of the marigold
Going ethereally green.

*continued*

*"wherever one gardens there is heartbreak "*

Working an autumn garden
It's not hard to think about dying
When the thinnest, most delicate
Of ices linger all morning
Here and there in the yellow grasses,

The sun on our back
Throws what is before us
Into a sharp relief
Snapdragon wither from
Stem to bud and dahlia from
The ruined blossom down

Fruits, leathery pods,
Nuts and berries,
A blizzard of seed,
Blights, rusts and smuts

The dry husks of the day
Like a fire going out,
Dying from its center
Burning clear at last.

*"every gardener knows the pleasures
of a pile of catalogs and a chair by the fire."*

No need of many earthy
Instructions here,
No thistle nor cursed soil,
No regions bereft of summer
Where hope is deferred
By every expectation blighted

*continued*

No white flowers and lanterns at evening,
No mottled rustle and ruin of Autumn
Leaves piled high against the door,
No charm wafted to a swarm of bees
No perennial huddling
Low against the bitter winter gale

No Spring passed
In anxious doubts and fears,
No green and leggy anticipation
In some privileged ignorance of
The hungrier facts of life.

*"siting a tree"*

The basic labor of an act
Of faith begun with patience
And prophesies of water
Wind and light, the earth
Turning darkly beneath you
Into something so high
So unlikely and full
Of bird and bird song

Some deep foreshadowing
Of some spring yet to be
In which to sit not complacently
In the sunny stretch
Of youth and expectancy
But in the cool old repose
Of one damn thing you did
When you meant to
So many years ago.

*continued*

*"what is a garden but a species of desire?"*

Which is why
When we first thought
Of paradise
We thought of a garden

And why lovers offer
Roses still without
Ever wondering why

And why the flower's
Dream of the future
Tight in its bud
Is the seed

Of the facing flower
That loves the light
And of the tart and thirsty

Spongy tongue of the root
Which hates it.

*"while it caters to our conceit to assume that flowers were created for our enjoyment, their true function is far more important."*

Bright bee flowers on a balmy day,
White odor of moth flowers
In the gray evening cast,

Blacker beetle flowers
Low to the ground and reeking
Of dung and meat,

*continued*

Lither wind flowers, reaching
With perfume and pattern
To all points of their compass

To the uglier bugs, and a few
Of the smaller birds,
And the briefer butterflies

Which the naive still believe
Are the souls of flowers swaying
In the easy breezes of desire.

# from This Day (1976- )

*"You are afraid whether you will rise from the dead or not, but you rose from the dead when you were born and didn't notice it."*

Boris Pasternak

# Foreigner

See him grunt and point.
See him with his big cold
body grunt and point.

Listen to him try
to talk like a person,
the way our words turn
to rubbish in his mouth.

Who could love him,
his face, a moon, his skin
the belly of the carp.

He walks like an ox.
He looks at the smallest thing
as if it were a miracle.

What a world that must be
the world that is his
where you can't ask for food
or tell a woman she's beautiful

where you can't pray or sing
or speak drunk to the dead
or cry out in the night for help.

# The Window

He chips at the salt on the sill
with a bloody nail, calls out
to passers-by who squint, look up,
agree abstractly and pass on.

Sometimes at night something weeps
inside him, something sits down
with its head in its hands
and smokes and stares.

A craving the color of morning
spirals within him,
its terraces are of conch and whelk,
its palms are open to the sun.

Who has unfolded this linen of dream
age and patience, this bay
open to the night?

# Gray Drapes

Gray drapes the shutterless room
when the sun goes beveling
the day we'd try to understand

even if we lived forever,
the moment we cling to
because it is our own.

The hand drawn more absently
towards pain, a flawless gesture,
floats or seems of itself no token.

Something goes on beyond the body,
that the body can believe,
the body knows itself, it fails.

Fear is the body's, fool,
the mind alone would go
anywhere, do anything.

Longing too is of the body,
the shape a hand makes, letting go,
the mouth slack, lips parted slightly.

# Calling It the Given
*full of quiet and regard*

The past you thought
would be over by now

a clamor in the heart
a paradise of ruins

its only regret is
it made you what you are

what used to be called
the future of the past

where the edges of the day
wear the day away to

the many worlds you
wake through towards

the world you'll wake in
in a moment.

# Like

a grief that one can cherish
or the dream aroused
the terrestrial version

the meaning and insinuation
of the signs of morning in
an eastern sky

a negative of the beautiful
or a movie of the future
running in reverse

of the shadow of the supple
apple saplings thrown
across the chop of shallow water

a leaf or a mountain
or the predictable horizon rising
to the repeatable moon.

# Pathetique

There is the sigh
that is too much
to do at work
he brings it home

it eats from the pan
with the only
clean spoon
more than its share

the sigh of the stew
of the onion
in its many skins
the sigh of bone

as it simmers
the many blind
and buried
sighs of potatoes.

# After Bonnefoy

I am surprised it took this long
for the fruit was in the tree
and the flat, nomadic light was
already leaning towards leaving.

Already the evening was easing
out of its shell – its eyes amber,
its chambered and fossorial heart.

Let painters have their first light,
a light like this unhinges us.
Prey to fever and incense ascending,
white bird off in high suspense
– light of evident things.

What's the soul without its flaws?
A moment without its
knowledge of death, unthinkable.

Sometimes it goes so clear in you
you can picture it
the slow nocturnal trellis' crawl,
a tractable past
which soothes you or does not

the day and the body that
the dead, if they awaken,
awaken singing.

## The Guest Room

Even without their story told,
more than a knickknack here and there,
a spoiled antimacassar,

some dried milkweed and dusty cattail
steeping for how long in a lidless teapot
a mysterious brew of nostalgia or regret,
or driftwood cast up on what huge tides
to settle here in winter on a prairie farm,

or grandfather's watch, stopped
ten minutes from now,
how many untold years ago?

A damp cloth across a dusty aspidistra,
a half-finished sampler,
"Oh Bear Me Away On your Snowy wings."

# The Lesson

Pay attention.
This is everything.
Pay attention.

# Counting

One is a slur of birds.
One is each bird, each wing.

One is also each leaf the birds scatter
as they swarm from one tree to another.

Who can say where one stops?
One could be an epic winter.

## The Idea of Soul

It shines as it rises
we say to the eyes.

It throbs, we tell the heart,
like a big morning star.

To the tips of the fingers
its touch would be exquisite.

# Bay View

*for Charlie*

If I had studied any lesson but the moment's lesson if I knew the proper names of trees or how a river chooses I'd find some shady spot along the bank and tell its thousand pages story.

But this is a public park where a shallow up-country river makes a little city pond I stop here often coming or going and I have noticed only how a pond broods its way through summer how in winter a pond is adamant in its silence.

How the heron waits on one delicate leg how the owl with silver at its talons and at wingtip listens as it looks and waits as water waits – after great motion, great pause.

As the sky must have once awaited the possibility of birds, or the earth, itself, its green impasse

# Bay View

Two hawks overhead one
soars off out of sight
one folds its wings
and drops into the trees,
off somewhere in the silence
a dove among the lilacs'
early perfume,
a loon with violet eyes
glides a pond all full of
the sky and its stillnesses,
a green dragonfly floats
downstream hits rock
scrambles up catches hold
and stays a long time,
its wings in the sun.

# Children

*Son*

I hear him crying
when he isn't here.
I know his face as my own.
He sits the way my grandfather sat.
He has the eyes of a woman
I've loved for a long time.
He reminds me of all
the wasted years
I imagined my father
couldn't love me enough.
He grows harder to carry
harder to put down every day.

*Second son*

You of winter
not springtime born
and more grasping at
my aging heart,
one with blue eyes
all alarm and habit
who among all
the gods is like you?
Fresh tenant
in yet another
story of my life,
one more gypsied boy
rescued from time,
who could imagine
one could love
so many and so much?

*continued*

*The only girl,*

the one with her eyes,
the one my mother wanted
but never got to see
whose mother wanted
her last and most
whose father saw
in those women's eyes
if not how long love lasts
then how it passes
sometimes through us
and sometimes
passes us by.

# Then

A vestigial
sadness astonishes
the fordable evening

someone taps
abstractly at the dial
of a luminous watch

the river falls
to other pools
other afternoons

what accident
a double cry goes out
what lunatic chore

small arms unmoored
by desire set out
upon an opposite shore.

# Strophe

By talons
it takes us
no matter where
we wander
how we wait
there is this
further blue
our longing
awakes in.

We think it quick
it is not it is
slow, a nest,
the deeper
the repose
the more emerges,
vast migrations
gather at this height.

## At the End Of the Road

For all our folding and unfolding,
the map's last panel is
neutral if untravelled ground
our sidelong eyes may meet
however tenuously between

hands as uneasy candles
caught up among opposing sighs
quick to point here no there
other birds beat their bright wings
under stars of other skies.

# Forgetting

Roughage of dreams, bits of string,
scrap of a list that marks my place
in an old romance I've just mislaid –
these the bird who steals
from birth feathers its nest with –
what always I'm forgetting –
why this place, why now, why I go on
calling after it thief, thief,
I don't know what you've stolen
so it burns in my hands as if gold.

# Shame

Shadows of birds fly before it
light leans towards its going
pain labors after its easing
down the hall out the screen door
through the trellis' lilt
the dark would-be roses going askew
along the ruined streets to the grasses
untangling as the river remembers its bank,
throw it away, throw it away again.

# Mine

You are with me this moment, now and again
when giddy heron eddy and stall,
when swans glide a glassy pond,
when a white gull opens another page of sky

when among the bushy silences of adolescent pines
the breast is opal, swathed in red flannel,
when in the houses on the hill full of their own
the egg is ivory, polished on a gray apron.

## For Dancing

Trembling in sympathy
unstroked by the bow
not the string played but
the string next to it

not music but what
in music makes us
wish we were dancing

in the present arms
of not forgotten lovers
whose sweep and purl
as midnight disappears

whose glide like that
lightly out of control
breathlessly unaware of
ability and will

whose reach of flesh
under fabric whose wanton
body of a beautiful youth
ever eager in our arms.

# Arabesque

The suns our minds are
our bellies moons our eyes stars
in the heart's wide sky our
longing to fly above our
sorry our heavy body is.

Breath after breath
the hand holds and lets go
filling and emptying with
the moment that rises
and lies down within us
amidst a further desire.

Always out of reach just
beyond touch lies the other
the own seeking its own
the very body's body crying out.

## A Whole Day

with nothing to do
so that's what we do with it
morning hazy fog banking in
huffy gulls pacing the flats

a book not good but thick
untroubled on our lap
letters we mean to write
unwritten again and again

until the last of the mist burns
off into afternoon so we let it
plenty of time for too much
coffee and cigarettes until

the belly feels like lunch
so it's yesterday's daily bread
and a small handful of beans
ripened in the sunny garden

we wish to sleep so
sleep comes and goes lightly
as waking shadows crawl
towards a late supper

of ripening peach and pear
cheese we forgot we still had
and tea we thought we ought
to have saved for tomorrow.

# Poem

There are cornflowers in a blue vase
and a window with a remnant
of daylight sky receding through
fresh curtains pulled back
with bows of their own color.

There is green suntea steeping
in a bottle on the sill
and a familiar breeze
that's brought home today
a parcel of lilac and dogwood.

There's a porcelain thimble
afloat in the reflection of
the vase on the table
and a single thread is all
that keeps the silver needle
from embroidering the moon.

There's the too familiar robin,
the clown on the polished lawn,
smug and overfed again,
and the other, the dove,
the longed for, early at her calling
in the thickest of the trees.

# Lament

*after Transtromer*

He puts down his pen
it lies on the table
it lies on the table
he puts down his pen.

He makes tea with lemon
all day tea steeps
in a green pot
on the table beside his pen.

The cat sleeps and eats
in the dreams of the cat
the cat starts and leaps
after crickets in the dark.

## About the Author

Bruce Taylor's poetry, fiction and translations have appeared in such places as *Carve, The Chicago Review, The Exquisite Corpse, The Formalist, Light, The Nation, Nerve, The New York Quarterly, Poetry,* and *E2ink-1: the Best of the Online Journals.* Taylor has won awards and fellowships from the Bush Artist Foundation, Wisconsin Arts Board, the NEA, NEH, and Fulbright-Hayes. He is Professor of English at the University of Wisconsin – Eau Claire where he lives with his three children.

www.ingramcontent.com/pod-product-compliance
Lightning Source LLC
Chambersburg PA
CBHW071004080526
44587CB00015B/2340